SIGHT WORDS
3rd Grade Workbook
(Baby Professor Learning Books)

AGAINST

in opposition to (someone or something)

against

against

Use it in a sentence.

BLOCK

a solid piece of material (such as rock or wood) that has flat sides and is usually square or rectangular in shape

block

block

Use it in a sentence.

CHANCE

an opportunity to do something;
an amount of time or a situation in
which something can be done

chance

chance

Use it in a sentence.

cows, bulls, or steers that are kept on
a farm or ranch for meat or milk

cattle

cattle

Use it in a sentence.

CHEW

to use your teeth to cut food into small
pieces before you swallow it

chew

chew

Use it in a sentence.

the course or path on which
something is moving or pointing

direction

direction

Use it in a sentence.

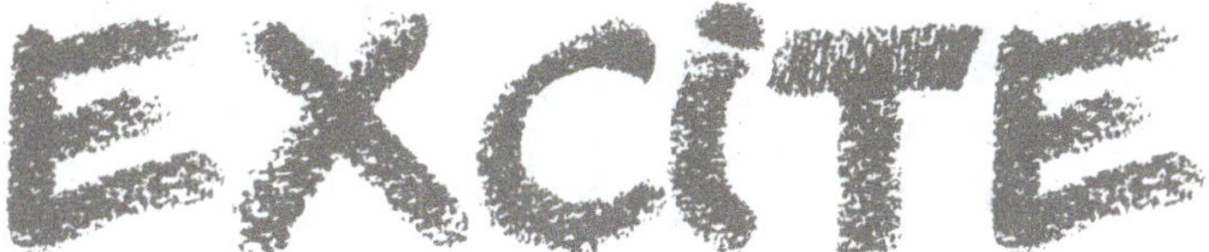

to cause feelings of enthusiasm in (someone); to make (someone) feel energetic and eager to do something

excite

excite

Use it in a sentence.

to search for something or someone
very carefully and thoroughly

hunt

hunt

Use it in a sentence.

as a substitute or equivalent

instead

instead

Use it in a sentence.

a person holding an academic degree higher
than a bachelor's but lower than a doctor's

master

master

Use it in a sentence.

PACKAGE

a box or large envelope that is sent
or delivered usually through the mail
or by another delivery service

package

package

Use it in a sentence.

QUITE

to a very noticeable degree or extent

quite

quite

Use it in a sentence.

to be left when the other parts are
gone or have been used

remain

remain

Use it in a sentence.

SPEND

to use (money) to pay for something

spend

spend

Use it in a sentence.

a natural flow of water that is smaller than a river

stream

stream

Use it in a sentence.

to say words in order to express your thoughts,
feelings, opinions, etc., to someone

speak

speak

Use it in a sentence.

SPREAD

to open, arrange, or place
(something) over a large area

spread

spread

Use it in a sentence.

STRETCH

to make (something) wider or longer by pulling it

stretch

stretch

Use it in a sentence.

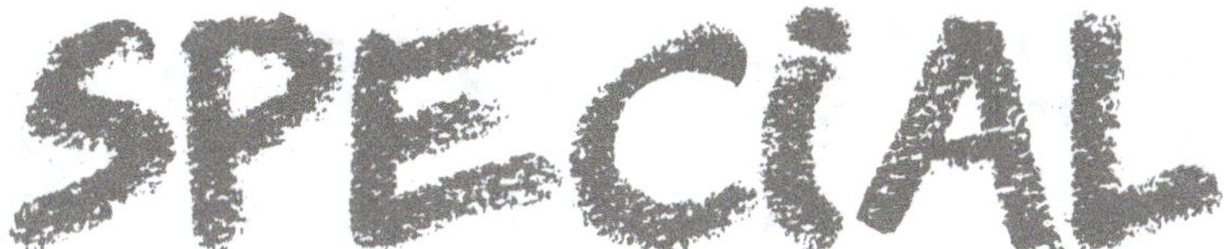

SPECIAL

different from what is normal or usual

special

special

Use it in a sentence.

happening, coming, or done very quickly
in a way that is usually not expected

suddenly

suddenly

Use it in a sentence.

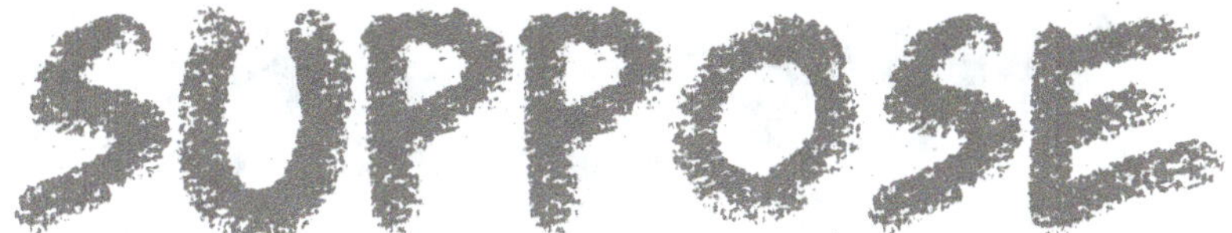

to think of (something) as happening or being
true in order to imagine what might happen

suppose

suppose

Use it in a sentence.

a group of people who compete in a sport, game, etc., against another group

team

team

Use it in a sentence.

to go on a trip or journey; to go to a place
and especially one that is far away

travel

travel

Use it in a sentence.

involving people or groups working
together to achieve something

united

united

Use it in a sentence.

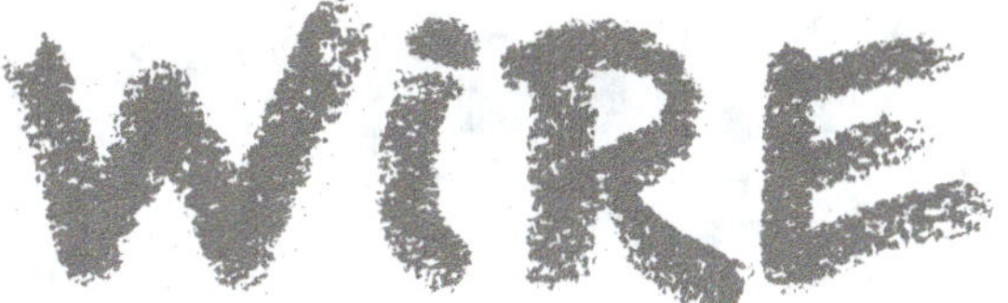

a thin, flexible thread of metal

wire

wire

Use it in a sentence.

less pleasant, attractive, appealing,
effective, useful, etc.

worse

worse

Use it in a sentence.

which one of the two

whether

whether

Use it in a sentence.

to tell (someone) about possible danger or trouble

warn

warn

Use it in a sentence.

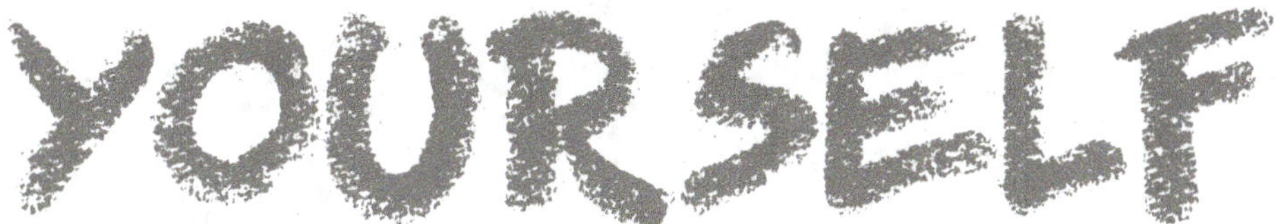

your normal or healthy self

yourself

yourself

Use it in a sentence.

Visit
BABY PROFESSOR
EDUCATION KIDS
www.BabyProfessorBooks.com
to download Free Baby Professor eBooks
and view our catalog of new and exciting
Children's Books